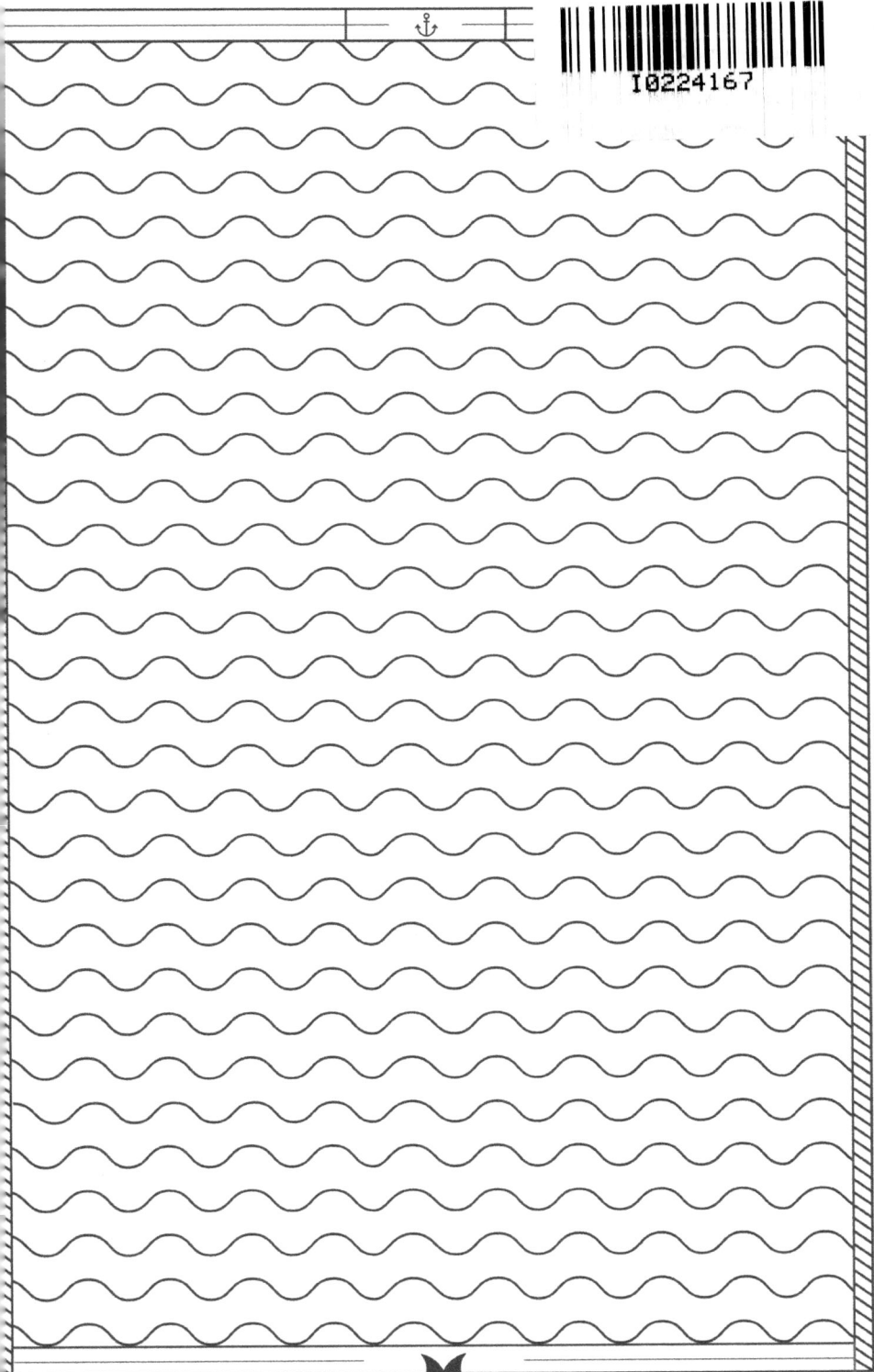

LATE TIDE

ROWENA HILL

MAREA TARDIVA

ITALIAN VERSION BY SILVIO MIGNANO

MAREA TARDÍA

'Alliteration

LATE TIDE | ROWENA HILL
Italian translated from the Spanish by Silvio Mignano
First edition in English in July, 2021

© Rowena Hill
© For the foreword Silvio Mignano
© Alliteration Publishing, 2021

Design by Elisa Barrios
Cover by Andrea Martínez
Editorial Coordination by Amayra Velón

ISBN: 979-8-9852666-0-3

THE SLOW DIGESTION OF WORDS

Note on *Marea tardía* by Rowena Hill
Silvio Mignano

In a passage of *Il fu Mattia Pascal (The Late Mattia Pascal)*, the novel (1904) by the Italian writer and dramatist Luigi Pirandello, Nobel Prize for literature in 1934, the protagonist, who no longer wants to be called Mattia Pascal but Adriano Meis, attends a production of Sofocles' *Electra* acted by automatic puppets. Mattia/Adriano is mystified by the novelty, which reveals brutally the concept of fiction in classical tragedy, and tries to imagine what would happen if Orestes, at the moment of avenging his father's death, noticed that the sky was simply a paper curtain, and torn besides.

In *Leap*, the second poem in Rowena Hill's new book, "At the back of the day's stage/ behind a threadbare black curtain/ fractions of figures gesticulate". They are her former teachers, these images, or figures, or fractions of figures, explain to the poet, and they add: "Feel how we pull your strings". Precisely, we would say, like a puppet, like one of the puppets acting the *Electra* that the late Mattia Pascal watches.

Fiction, in the sense closest to Borges, is the thread that holds *Marea tardía* together. The sea is not the sea, it's a mental construction that can be reached through a trap door in a cellar: it's a sea below the sea, agitated by currents and waves that move the reader's memory, obliging him to rethink his own existential certainties, which will no longer look so certain and solid.

In the same way, the eye is not simply the organ of sight from an anatomical point of view, but a window we look through to see our lives *à rebours*. They will be transformed into plays for the theatre and over the stage vultures, cats, clouds, pigeons and butterflies will parade - puppets, once again, which are no longer what they appear but something else, characters that embody feelings, memories, fragments of existence.

Rowena Hill resides in two languages, English and Spanish, in a plurality of cultures and in a reality, that of Venezuela, which in its turn is a cauldron of human and cultural identities and heritages and an eternal frontier territory between different worlds. She writes and translates, Rowena, and so is uniquely familiar with the ambiguity of the word, which is also its strength and richness. A word doesn't always have the first meaning that comes to mind when we read or listen to it, and no one knows it better than a translator.

So, a blue plastic bag blowing in the dust of an empty street is not necessarily what we think; it can announce a band of haggard goblins that have taken over a city reduced to debris and waste. A feeling of deep pity runs through the book, together with the intimate pain that memory causes the poet. She feels no hypocritical shame in showing us her nostalgia for the instincts that are still alive in her body, and yet no longer match what they were: she does this through verses with a simple, apparently banal structure, which however are dense and sometimes need a long time to be truly read and above all digested.

But it is not a happy metamorphosis that these poems by Rowena Hill offer us: they are not only a cathartic reflection on existence and its transformation in time. The last part of the book takes on desolate tones: little space remains for any redemption, in a reality where the crematorium is a shining bread oven and the alternative to burning is the body slipping, without a coffin, toward the blind depths of the sea - once again, the metaphorical sea that opens up in our inner consciousness.

It's the expression of a grief that's no longer only personal but also collective, where the Towers of Silence of the Parsis in India become a titanic funeral scaffold, an impossible stretcher from whose giddy height the bodies fall toward the abyss. So it's perhaps no longer a puppeteer that's pulling the strings of the characters on stage: it may be the Parcae, the Fates, and instead their action is to cut those strings.

A powerful synthesis between the images of the puppeteer and the Parcae is Thanatos, who arrives at the end of the book as an executioner and at the same time a liberator, subtly in balance between tenderness and violence, tragedy and humor. Rowena Hill's voice reaches from this moment on perhaps its highest level: at the point where there are no frontiers between human feelings, where fear and hope annul each other and converge, leaving the field open for the most enduring existential questions, for the word and its indefinable protean nature.

LATE TIDE

I

GROUNDSWELL

Conversion

Scratching of rat claws in the cellar
swells to percussion,
random pulses on the sea bottom
collide in a quake,
scattered sparks gather
in a lightning flash,
expose the god's face
the hand with the dagger.

Leap

At the back of the day's stage
behind a threadbare black curtain
fractions of figures gesticulate.
"We're your masters," they murmur,
"since childhood we've taught you to spit, to pray.
Feel how we pull your strings."

"I don't feel it," I answer
and push them aside to pass
into an empty room
where silence is a yell
with no exit till I find
a trap door in the floor.

I jump into the void,
in the thick dark my fingers brush
winged seeds of words.

Sea Below the Sea

In a cellar of the psyche
a sea below the sea
lit by a deathly glow
an eclipse; on the beach
no creature lives.

I walk along the edge of the silent waves
dreaming the birth in the foam
of cells and songs.

Suddenly the water divides
and objects are hurled out
fragments of lives and bodies
twisted cables splinters of furniture
broken wings drowned fishes
and hairy legs skulls with threads
knots of guts and veins
that twist and wriggle on the sand.

I wish, I want
from my deepest heart
to assemble the debris
reunite the shards
of the world that belongs to me.

But I'm useless, dumb
and in my resignation I taste peace
while the light fades.

I efface myself, but the light?
It wasn't dawn, it was dusk,
it's gone. And those eyes
that radiate in the ground?

Groundswell

Agitation - the dictionary says -
spreading from inside.
It comes to beaches in big waves
that threaten strollers
and bring to light
the ferments of the sea floor.

FLOWERS

I lived in flowers
lost in the heart of their trumpets
pierced by their lances
shining in their suns.

Later I descended stems
and thick trunks,
swam in tides of sap.

Now with roots
I sink in the original clay
the dark humus that germinates
and molders.

INTO THE BOWELS

I want to return to the cellar
where I belong.
The cat is lying beside me,
the neatness of her striped orange fur
absorbs me, she yawns
and the barbed porcelain
of her teeth marks the channel
down her dark throat.

I turn to the Sanskrit dictionary,
one word - *vyoman* - leads me
round objects and domains
- sky and water, cow and jewel,
the absurdity of a flower growing in air -
of an intense remote life,
the letters and their resonance
sink me in the black loam
where language germinates.

THINKING OF SANSKRIT

The leaves of the word leaf
are a second birth,
behind are the veined green rags
mutating with the slant of the light.

****

Struggling with syntax
baffled by conjugations
the eye suddenly perceives
how an enormous whale
rises from the sea of sounds
that strive to articulate
constellating them in its bulk.

****

Any letter of an alphabet
picked out chewed over in amazement
leads to the skin of the same
infinitely dense pregnant toxic
body of language.

****

The leaves that fall nameless
the clouds that file gauzily
through a demented or ecstatic eye
lead to the open sea
pure liquid without order
without time, terror
or animal bliss.

THE POLES

for Igor Barreto

To prepare to ascend
K2 in the winter,
to desire a season of pain
as pure and intense
as the steppes of snow
white to the bones' marrow
to the skull's inner walls
beyond all certainty
or hope -

is it equal to the courage
of the poet who opens his body
to all the human misfortunes
of his ruinous age
articulating them like rocks in the field
round the hidden summit,
the unscathed good?

II

THE KNOT

The first substance
the spontaneous birthing
without cause or relation
of the mother void
is light.

For uncountable generations
it's incubated in the cells
of all creatures,
it converses with the light in the sky.

The eyes are its door.

At the moment of death
when the heart's knot is loosened
and our bulk unravels,
will what's left be light free again?
Is that we reduce to
essential borderless light?
or do we retrace the last passage?
is the beginning annulled with us
in nothingness?

TESTIMONY OF THE EYE

The Window

I am the eye,
I'm the only thing I can't see,
on a clear day I can sweep the horizon,
I watch a vine's tendrils wind upward
or the pimples ripen under a man's beard.

In the other direction I see bile rising
in the body that sustains me
and the proliferating architecture of dreams.

I'm hinge
I'm membrane
I'm camera,
sometimes I'm very tired,
I can become opaque in either direction,
one day I'll swivel and cease.

TRIPTYCHS

The three parts of the same egg-shaped instant
divided for intellect's sake
into outside inside and screen
must be restored to their shell
seamlessly amalgamated
for light to abound there
and memory take hold.

Eye meets world,
shapes and textures
depths and movements
stamp their unique constellation
on a moist retina,
perfectly received
the blaze of that juncture
is free of time.

Names adhere
it may be a nanosecond later
then hands chest hair
and powerful feet,
gods and goddesses
turn the elements into stories
harness love and fear.

Eye trembles with the draught
blowing from heart and nerves
perceives the flux of juices
their oscillations
and the colors rising from viscera
emotions in flower.

expanse of heaving water
blue breaking into white
the wind lashes

Her rest is broken
she stirs uneasy
and spits reproaches
into the throat
of the exciter.

An inner tide
swells and effervesces
in rasping streaks.

vulture erect on the rooftree
bare head swiveling
wings spread to the sun

Black angel
the vulture rests
from its work as scavenger
its purifying hunger.

Disgust at its wrinkled
grey bald pate
dissolves in sympathy
for its human gestures.

dusk at the garden's edge
yellow daisies retain
daylight

Flowers glow like lanterns
for late foragers
still holding the darkness
at bay.

Primal pleasure
heart's applause
for light blooming
against the dark

wind sways the forest
loose leaves spin
to the mottled ground

An ancient breath
commands the trees
changing seasons
like keys in music.

The movements of a dance
prick and rise along limbs
shake with the assault of autumn.

the cat stares
its eyes are circles
shining and still

A little god
regards the object
fur may quiver
paws contract
gaze is unmoving
sight in stone.

Hand reaching for softness
may be clawed for disrespect,
muscles clench and release.

shattered motorcycle
lies half under a truck
stain spreads on asphalt

From how far back
did Fate pull the strings
of this collision?
Did the rider see
the blade fall?

Flesh shrinks and trembles
fragile and soft
guessing the impact
of hurled metal.

cloud patterns
streak the sky
from edge to edge

An artist's hand
has covered the vault
with white feathers.

Eyes look upward,
heart and breath
surge after them
into foaming space.

crammed into lines
men and women wait
in the dirty street

A false godling
fat and flabby
has condemned them to empty shelves
and a diet of lies.

The heart constricts
with pity
and shame stirs with anger
at their impotence.

sequence of precise forms
a pigeon lands
on a cornice

The shapes god used
to articulate creation
triangle circle square
alternate from wall to wall,
the flight of a pigeon
disturbs the symmetry.

Envy a bird's sleekness
the freedom to flutter
not knowing it inhabits
splendor.

a dying cockroach
shiny brown shell
waves feeble legs

The species built to last
a million years
throws its members away
crunchy underfoot
and multiplies
and multiplies.

Disgust tingles
in nose and lips
crawls in stomach and thighs,
compassion peels away,
feet are ready to stamp.

a blue plastic bag
drifts in the dust
of the empty street

The gods have deserted,
the city belongs now
to the haggard goblins
of debris and waste.

A hole in the belly
opens and swallows
faith in the future
daily cheer.

a tiny iridescent beetle
clings to a yellow rose
devouring it

Life feeds on life,
it was established so
by an ambivalent creator
his notion of balance.

The heart revolts but knows
such fierce closeness
is a kind of love.

III

MOURNING

My house no longer is
my home, shelter, rock,
dwelling around a fountain.
Its mute guardians fled
when the last tree on the border
was felled by the invaders;
its transparent sphere exploded,
the shards of its silence float
over the parched garden
fall at night on the roof
the tread of a wounded animal.

The elastic organ
that was I has been torn,
the movements of a scattered dance
have stiffened.

The dream of roundness I brought with me
shatters, leaves the hollow;
sometimes it knows itself in a splinter.

BAG OF BONES

I lay down my head,
I don't feel the softness
of my padded flesh
merging with the pillow
but a hard container
that can't settle.

I jump and the springs
of my legs don't cushion
the rattling bag of bones,
the slightest scratch
tears my cheap paper skin
and watery blood oozes.

The places of desire
are still marked on my body
but their heat is waning
and at the seats of generation
- crown, throat, heart -
a rainbow sometimes wavers.

If the sun is favorable
the bundle can still feel whole.

MATRIOSKA

The closest wrapping
is skin;
I look through its orifices.

Clothes are next,
dulling me
or interpreting my shine.

House is a carapace
riddled
with worries.

City, country, world
are cages
shabby and shared.

The most spacious cocoon
that adheres to me
is the weather,
lights and shadows the fibers
of my sky.

Does the onion squeal
when it's stripped
to its empty core?

This yellow butterfly
has no more layers to cast off.
It's pure being.

ELEMENT WATER

i
Is the river in the warm afternoon
a portrait of a hidden dimension
of my body?
In the falls the blood runs fast
recovering the beat of earlier years;
further down it slips dividing
around rocks and fallen branches
like vessels in the brain
seeking illuminations;
in pools it mirrors sleep.

ii
The cold white current
breaks through my borders
penetrates my pores,
in the impetus
in my body's heat
water and blood become
one thing
a vein of earth.

iii
Bleed me I beg you,
cut my right arm
and bind it so feverish action
ceases and the force it carried
pours out splashing the earth red
and leaving me pale and limp
not answerable to desire.

IV

*Sometimes it seems to us that what is mysterious
about the mystery of this mystery
is based on a misunderstanding,
and that the misunderstanding is produced
by our complication;
without knowing what it consists of,
we feel that it must be something very simple,
simple like the solutions of life and love.*

VLADIMIR JANKÉLÉVITCH

AND STILL...

i
Light has stagnated in the eye
sounds are reduced to borborygmus
the skeleton makes its rounds
from posture to posture
in different places
while time passes colorless.

ii
A branch of very green leaves
wiped away a veil,
suddenly time is changed
flesh has consistency
the light is an instant stolen
from surrounding nothing
from death waiting.

ASTROLOGY

The calculation of astral influences
their combinations and disjunctions
unfolds ad infinitum
while the subject of the horoscope
is no longer there.

The groundswell of appetites
sublime or wicked projects
illusions still growing
even in decrepitude
tows into a future
that doesn't exist.

Time incarnated in organs
irregular and pitiless
could warn of the truth
but it's blind and dumb.

At every moment my being
resuscitates from the abyss.

For how long?

CREMATORIUM

Stone speaks the accomplishment
of my mineral soul,
further inside is only fire.

It's not hell though it's streaked
by the dark iridescence
of Lucifer's eye
and roars like the conflagration
of the plague-ridden city;
it swells and shatters fevers
then glows like a bread oven
or the fresh sun of morning.

In the end there are embers
and absolute light.

NO COFFIN

Thorny winds blow
over the towers of silence
sweeping away cells and hairs
bracing the powerful wings
of vultures that will perch
to tear the corpse apart.

Arms and legs burn
as fiercely as logs
if the pyre is tall
and there is plenty of oil,
the roar is deafening:
holocaust of one that culminates
in the skull exploding.

Wrapped in canvas like a mummy
the body slips off the stretcher
and dives into the sea.
Water erodes the shroud,
salt softens the deserted flesh,
what's left is a packet of bones
on the blind floor.

Earth thrown falls
on extinguished eyes
invades the half-open mouth
crushes the breast
compresses the sides
while the flesh liquefies
helped by worms
and becomes one substance
with earth.

The fifth element
is space
between galaxies
between the particles of atoms
in a flower or a brain,
so nearly nothing
won't it connect us to the beyond?
would not that fusion
be eternal life?

The universe doesn't answer.
We fill space with angels
and desiring spirits.

THUG DEATH

Thug death arrives
defenseless and hurt.

On a strip that opens
between the face of darkness
and the final breath
trapped voices moan
complain laugh bitterly
demand forgiveness or revenge,
a live recording in the void.

Unhappy the mediums
who pick up their lamentations,
they're shaken to the marrow
and risk erasure.

THE THANATOSES

Mister Thanatos

You, sir, live (or don't live)
on a spectral frontier
between unthinkable nothing
and all the rest.

Don't your toes in a careless moment
ever disappear
on the other side?
How do you pull them back
- whole or decomposed -
to this shore where you don't exist
except virtually?

I don't deny your power,
in coitus in prayer in bread
your sentry box stands,
wanting to or dreading it
we're all going toward you.

Even the tiger.
When the marvel of blazing stripes
and fierce claws approaches
don't you feel sorry to smash it
against that hypothetical wall?

The day it's my dogs' turn
to (un)know the last crossing
receive them please with kindness,
shove them softly
into that silence.

THANATOS'S HOUSE

Thanatos's house spreads
over a small rise
just a few steps from the wall
of compact darkness.

Treasures and knick-knacks
stuff the rooms
beads manuscripts chests
maybe an old shoe
tons of coins,
in a stable pets are lying
and even babies,
objects that the dying
wanted to take to the afterlife
and that froze here
by the force of their desire.
The ones left to their heirs
are reproductions.

Thanatos enjoys his furniture
looking in the windows,
he has no time to enter.
He never sleeps.

THANATOS'S WIFE

Thanatos's wife
sleeps in her alcove,
the bed is soft and flowery,
her face peeps from a nest
of silk and velvet,
she breathes quietly.

Sometimes her skin is smooth
and her eyelids tender
like a newborn;
then her lips redden
her hair quivers:
does she hope to be awakened
by the voice of love?

At an unknown hour
finally she opens her eyes
in her brown wrinkled face,
she smiles with entire compassion
at the stunned passer-by
as if saying my embrace
is the promise that accompanies you
up to the limit.

THANATOS, THE FAMILY

For people dragged off
by a wanton death
without decorum or speeches
Thanatos changes his person
multiplies his appearances
sudden and temporary offspring.

Dwarf Thanatos signals
to the crippled and maimed
to beings mangled by death
who see their own intestines:
trust me, he shouts,
I know that at the final moment
of light you'll have restored
heroic limbs
unbounded sight.

Clod Thanatos bends down
holds out his hairy hand
to the weary who are rotting inside
who don't know what's happening to them
and have seen no doctor.
Welcome cancers, he says,
welcome fungal sores,
we're all made of the same substance
growing light here in peace.

Almost transparent blue
a *Thanatos lad*
sprouts in the sea
beside the drowning baby

yellow and hunchbacked
for the child that perishes
while crossing the desert.

Grey as lead the platoon
of *Thanatos gnomes*
that serve in the rubble
of bombed cities.

They vanish as quickly as they crystallized
as quickly as the brief journeys
they escort are extinguished
each with its own sense.

V

WITHOUT...

Shadows are lovely
in the day's round
ubiquitous companions
that ask for nothing
and will desert me.

The light inside a lily
over the peaks at evening
in the cat's hairs
is lent them by my eyes
and I won't sustain it.

The body declines
the chassis of a destiny corrodes
while the brain turns off synapses;
when it becomes an inert grey mass
where will its light be?

Without shadows
without a flower
without a brain,
will a strand of light
recognize me?

MAREA TARDIVA

TRADUZIONE DI SILVIO MIGNANO

LA LENTA DIGESTIONE DELLE PAROLE

Nota su *Marea tardiva* di Rowena Hill
Silvio Mignano

In un passo de *Il fu Mattia Pascal*, il romanzo del 1904 dello scrittore e drammaturgo italiano Luigi Pirandello, Premio Nobel per la letteratura nel 1934, il protagonista, che già non risponde più al nome di Mattia Pascal bensì a quello di Adriano Meis, assiste a una messa in scena dell'*Elettra* di Sofocle interpretata da marionette automatiche. Mattia/Adriano è sconcertato dalla novità, che mette a nudo brutalmente il concetto di finzione nella tragedia classica, e prova a immaginare che cosa accadrebbe se Oreste, sul punto di vendicare la morte del padre, si accorgesse che il cielo è semplicemente un telone di carta, e per giunta lacerato.

In *Salto*, la seconda poesia di questo nuovo libro di Rowena Hill, "in fondo allo scenario dei giorni / dietro un telone nero lacerato / gesticolano frazioni di figure". Sono i suoi antichi maestri, le spiegano le immagini o figure, e aggiungono: "non senti come tiriamo i tuoi fili?". Proprio, verrebbe da dire, come a una marionetta, come una delle marionette dell'*Elettra* cui assiste il fu Mattia Pascal.

La finzione, nel senso più borgesiano, è il filo conduttore di *Marea tardiva*. Il mare non è mare, è una costruzione mentale alla quale si giunge attraverso una botola in una soffitta: è un mare sotto il mare, agitato da correnti e onde che smuovono la memoria del lettore, obbligandolo a ripensare alle proprie certezze esistenziali, che ormai non gli appariranno più tanto certe, né così ferme.

Allo stesso modo l'occhio non è semplicemente l'organo della vista in una prospettiva anatomica, ma una finestra alla quale ci affacciamo per vedere *à rebours* le nostre vite. Queste saranno trasformate in pièce teatrali e sulla scena sfileranno avvoltoi, gatti, nuvole, colombe e farfalle – marionette, una volta ancora, che non sono quel che sembrano ma tutt'altra cosa, personaggi che incarnano sentimenti, memorie, frammenti dell'esistenza.

Rowena Hill vive appartenendo a due lingue, l'inglese e lo spagnolo, e immersa in una pluralità di culture, in una realtà, quella venezuelana, che è a sua volta un crogiolo di identità ed eredità umane e culturali, un'eterna terra di frontiera tra mondi diversi. Scrive e traduce, Rowena, e possiede allora una familiarità unica con l'ambiguità della parola, che ne è anche la forza e la ricchezza. Una parola non ha sempre necessariamente il primo significato che ci viene alla mente quando la leggiamo o ascoltiamo, e non c'è nessuno che lo sappia meglio di un traduttore.

Così, una busta di plastica azzurra che gira nella polvere di una strada vuota non è per forza quello che crediamo che sia, può annunciare una pattuglia di spiriti smagriti che si impossessano di una città fatta scoria e rovina. Un sentimento di profonda pena attraversa il libro, accompagnato dal dolore che suscita la memoria nell'intimo della poetessa. Questa non ha alcun pudore ipocrita a mostrarci il rimpianto per gli istinti che ancora sopravvivono nel suo corpo ma che tuttavia non corrispondono più a quelli che furono: lo fa con versi che hanno una struttura semplice, apparentemente banale, e che invece sono densi e a volte richiedono un lungo tempo per leggerli davvero e soprattutto per digerirli.

Non è tuttavia una metamorfosi felice, quella che queste poesie così filosofiche di Rowena Hill ci presentano: non c'è solamente una riflessione catartica sull'esistenza e sulla sua trasformazione nel tempo. La parte finale del libro assume toni desolati: resta poco spazio per qualsiasi redenzione, in una realtà nella quale il crematorio è un forno per il pane che risplende, e l'alternativa alla combustione è lo scivolar giù del corpo, privo anche di urna, verso la profondità cieca del mare – ancora una volta, il mare metaforico che si apre nelle nostre più intime coscienze.

È l'espressione di un lutto non più soltanto personale ma anche collettivo, nel quale le Torri del silenzio usate dai Parsi in India si trasformano in una titanica impalcatura funebre, un'impossibile barella dalla cui altezza vertiginosa i corpi cadono verso l'abisso. Allora non sarà più forse un burattinaio a manipolare i fili dei personaggi sullo scenario, potrebbero essere invece le parche, e il loro gesto sarà dunque piuttosto quello di tagliare quei fili.

Una sintesi potente tra le immagini del burattinaio e delle parche è Thanatos, che giunge alla fine del libro come un boia ma allo stesso tempo come un liberatore, in sottile equilibrio tra dolcezza e violenza, tragedia e umorismo. La voce di Rowena Hill arriva forse in questo momento al suo punto più alto: quello nel quale non ci sono più confini tra i sentimenti umani, nel quale la paura e la speranza si annullano e convergono, lasciando campo libero alle più eterne domande esistenziali, alla parola e alla sua indefinibile natura proteiforme.

MAREA TARDIVA

I

MARE MOSSO

La conversione

Il graffiare di topi in cantina
diventa percussione,
battiti aleatori in fondo al mare
sbattono e fanno tremare,
scintille disperse si fondono
in un lampo,
rivelano il volto del dio
la mano con la daga.

Salto

Al fondo dello scenario dei giorni,
dietro un telone nero consunto
gesticolano frazioni di figure.
«Siamo i tuoi maestri», sussurrano,
«fin dall'infanzia t'insegnammo a sputare, a pregare,
non senti come tiriamo i tuoi fili?».

«Non lo sento», rispondo
e le metto da parte
in una stanza vuota
dove il silenzio è urlo
senza uscita finché scopro
una botola nel pavimento.

Salto senza vedere il suolo,
nella spessa oscurità le mie dita a tentoni
toccano semi alati di parole.

Mare sotto il mare

In una cantina della psiche,
un mare sotto il mare
illuminato da una luce cadaverica,
da eclisse, sulla spiaggia,
non vive nessun essere.

Cammino sul bordo delle onde silenziose
sognando il parto tra la spuma
di cellule e canti.

All'improvviso si apre l'acqua
e cominciano a uscire gettati
frammenti di vita e corpi
cavi ritorti schegge di mobili
ali spezzate pesci annegati
e gambe marcite crani sfilacciati
nodi di viscere e di vene:
si ritorcono e muovono sulla sabbia.

Io voglio, desidero
dal più profondo di me stessa
assemblare i resti
ricomporre i frantumi
del mondo che mi appartiene.

Ma sono incapace, muta
e nella resa assaporo la pace
mentre la luce si dissipa.

Io mi cancello, ma la luce?
Non era l'alba, era crepuscolo,
andato via. E questi occhi
che irradiano il suolo?

Mare mosso

Agitazione – dice il dizionario – [1]
propagata dall'interno.
Arriva alla spiaggia a grandi ondate
che minacciano i passanti
e fanno uscire a risplendere
i fermenti del fondo.

---

[1] In italiano manca un termine esattamente corrispondente al mar de fondo o
mar de leva spagnolo, che la Real Academia de España nel suo dizionario defi-
nisce così: "1. s.m. o f. Agitazione delle acque del mare propagata dall'interno e
che in forma attenuata raggiunge i luoghi più vicini alla costa. Può anche prodursi
in mare aperto senza effetti sulle coste, con propagazione di onde, anche deboli,
da un luogo all'altro. 2. s.m. o f. Inquietudine o agitazione più o meno latente che
intorbidisce o rende difficile il corso di un qualsiasi evento".

I FIORI

Ho vissuto i fiori
perdendomi nel cuore delle loro trombe
trapassata dalle loro lance
brillando nei loro soli.

Poi sono scesa per i talli
e i tronchi massicci,
nuotavo nelle maree di savia.

E ora con le radici
affondo nel fango della fonte
l'oscuro humus che germina
e scompone.

VERSO LE VISCERE

Voglio tornare nella cantina
che mi appartiene.
La gatta si sdraia accanto a me,
la pulcritudine del pelo arancio e bianco
mi cattura, sbadiglia
e la porcellana appuntita
dei denti segna il canale
verso la gola scura.

Ricorro al dizionario di sanscrito,
una parola – *vyoman* – mi porta a spasso
tra oggetti e dimensioni
– cielo e acqua, vacca e gioiello,
l'assurdo di un fiore che cresce in aria –
di una vita intensa remota,
le lettere e la loro risonanza
mi affondano nella terra nera
dove germina il linguaggio.

PENSANDO IL SANSCRITO

Le foglie della parola foglia
sono una seconda nascita,
dietro ci sono i panni verdi venati
che mutano quando la luce si polarizza.

****

Combattendo con la sintassi
stordito dalle coniugazioni
l'occhio all'improvviso percepisce
come una balena enorme
sorge dal mare dei suoni
che cercano di enunciare,
costellandoli.

****

Qualsiasi lettera di un alfabeto
separata farfugliata con stupore
conduce alla pelle dello stesso corpo
infinitamente denso gravido
tossico del linguaggio.

****

Le foglie che cadono senza nome
le nubi che sfilano vaporose
nell'occhio demente o estasiato
portano al mare aperto
pura liquidità senz'ordine
senza tempo, terrore
o godimento animale.

I POLACCHI

A Igor Barreto

Prepararsi all'ascesa
del K2 in inverno,
desiderare una stagione di dolore
puro e intenso
come le steppe di neve
bianca fino al midollo delle ossa
fino alle pareti interne del cranio
più in là di ogni certezza
o speranza:

equivale al coraggio
del poeta che apre il corpo
a tutte le disgrazie umane
e della sua epoca oscura
articolandole come rocce tutt'intorno
alla cima nascosta
il bene incolume?

II

IL NODO

La prima sostanza
il parto spontaneo
senza causa o relazione
del nulla madre
è la luce.

Fino a generazioni senza numero
è incubata nelle cellule
di tutte le creature,
conversa con la luce del cielo.

Gli occhi sono la sua porta.

Al momento della morte
quando si scioglie il nodo nel petto
e le strutture si smontano
quel che resta sarà di nuovo la luce libera?
a questo ci riduciamo:
luce essenziale e senza frontiere?
o ripercorriamo l'ultimo passaggio?
si annulla insieme a noi il principio
nel nulla?

TESTIMONIANZE DELL'OCCHIO

La finestra

Io sono l'occhio
sono l'unico che non vedo
in un giorno senza nubi setaccio l'orizzonte
guardo i viticci che si arrampicano da una vite
o maturare i brufoli sotto una barba.

Al contrario vedo crescere la bile
nel corpo che mi sostiene
e l'architettura proliferante dei sogni.

Sono cardine
sono membrana
sono fotocamera
a volte mi stanco troppo
posso diventare opaco nelle due direzioni
un giorno mi girerò e smetterò.

TRITTICI

Le tre parti dello stesso istante ovoidale
diviso in nome dell'intelletto
in fuori dentro e schermo
devono essere rimesse dentro il guscio
amalgamate senza cuciture
perché lì la luce abbondi
e la memoria metta radici.

L'occhio incontra il mondo,
forme e testure
profondità e movimenti
imprimono la sua costellazione unica
nella retina morbida,
perfettamente ricevuta
la fiamma di questa congiuntura
è libera dal tempo.

I nomi si aggiungono
forse un nanosecondo più tardi,
poi mani petto capelli
e poderosi piedi,
dei e dee
trasformano gli elementi in storie
sottomettono amore e paura.

L'occhio trema nella corrente
che soffia da cuore e nervi
percepisce il flusso degli umori
le loro oscillazioni
e i colori che emanano le viscere.

onde accavallate
azzurro si frange bianco
il vento flagella

Il suo riposo si interrompe
si agita disturba
sputa rimproveri
nella gola
del perturbatore.

Una marea intima
cresce e ribolle
con venature catarrose.

zamuro[2] fermo sulla sommità
testa pelata che ruota
ali distese al sole

Angelo nero
lo zamuro riposa
dal suo compito di necrofago
dalla sua fame che purga.

La repulsione per la sua calvizie
rugosa e grigia
si dissolve in simpatia
per i suoi gesti di persona.

---

2   Con il termine zamuro si indica popolarmente in Venezuela un grosso avvol-
toio che può appartenere sia alla specie Coragyps atratus (urubù dalla testa nera o
avvoltoio nero americano) sia a quella Cathartes aura (avvoltoio collorosso), en-
trambe rientranti nella famiglia Cathartidae, esclusiva delle Americhe.

crepuscolo al confine del giardino
margherite gialle trattengono
il chiarore del giorno

I fiori brillano come fari
per insetti ritardatari
tengono ancora lontane
le tenebre.

Stupore profondo
applauso del cuore
per la luce che fiorisce
contro la notte.

il vento culla la selva
foglie sciolte svolazzano
verso il terreno maculato

Un alito antico
domina gli alberi
cambiando stagioni
come chiavi nella musica.

I gesti di una danza
pungono e salgono alle estremità
scuotono con l'assalto dell'autunno.

il gatto guarda
i suoi occhi sono cerchi
brillanti e quieti

Un piccolo dio
fissa l'oggetto
il pelo può tremare
le unghie contrarsi
lo sguardo è immobile
pietra veggente.

La mano che cerca il morbido
per dispetto può essere graffiata,
i muscoli si tendono e rilassano.

moto distrutta
finita sotto il camion
macchia che si espande sull'asfalto

Da che punto del passato
tirava il Destino i fili
di questa collisione?
Il conducente ha visto
cadere la spada?

La carne si stringe e trema
fragile e tenera
presente l'impatto
di metallo lanciato.

le nubi tracciano
scie nel cielo
da un margine all'altro

Una mano da artista
ha coperto la volta
di piume bianche.

La vista si alza,
cuore e respiro
si gettano dietro di lei
nello spazio spumoso.

accalcati in coda
uomini e donne in attesa
in strade immonde.

Un piccolo dio falso
grasso e flaccido
li ha condannati a scaffali vuoti
e a una dieta di menzogne.

Il dolore stringe
il cuore,
la vergogna si mescola alla rabbia
per l'impotenza.

sequenza di figure esatte
si posa una colomba
su un cornicione

Le forme che usò dio
per articolare la creazione
triangolo cerchio quadrato
si alternano da muro a muro,
il volo di una colomba
perturba questa simmetria.

Invidiate la levigatezza dell'uccello
la libertà del suo volo
senza che sappia
di abitare lo splendore.

uno scarafaggio moribondo
carapace brillante marrone
agita zampe deboli

La specie disegnata per durare
un milione di anni
scarta le sue membra
scricchiolanti sotto i piedi
e si moltiplica
e si moltiplica.

Pizzica il disgusto
in naso e labbra,
vengono brividi in ventre e cosce,
la compassione cessa,
il piede è pronto a calpestare.

una busta di plastica azzurra
gira nella polvere
della strada vuota

Gli dei hanno disertato,
la città appartiene adesso
agli spiriti smagriti
di rovine e rifiuti.

Un buco nello stomaco
s'apre e ingoia
la fede nel futuro
l'allegria quotidiana.

uno scarabeo iridescente minuto
si aggrappa a una rosa gialla
divorandola

La vita si nutre di vita,
in questo modo stabilì
un creatore ambivalente
la sua nozione di equilibrio.

Il cuore si ribella ma sa
che questa fierezza intima
è una specie di amore.

III

LUTTO

La mia casa non è più
la mia casa, rifugio, roccia
abitazione attorno a una fonte;
i suoi guardiani muti sono fuggiti
al cadere dell'ultimo albero di confine
abbattuto dagli invasori;
la sfera trasparente è scoppiata,
galleggiano i frammenti del suo silenzio
sul giardino rinsecchito,
cadono la notte sul tetto,
passi di animale ferito.

L'organo elastico
che ero io si è lacerato,
si sono accartocciati i gesti
di una danza dispersa.

Il sogno di rotondità che avevo portato
si frantuma, lascia un vuoto,
a volte si riconosce in una scheggia.

SACCO D'OSSA

Faccio riposare la testa,
non sento la morbidezza
della mia carne imbottita
che si fonde con il cuscino
ma un involucro duro
che non trova riposo.

Salto e le molle
delle mie gambe non ammortizzano
il tintinnare del sacco d'ossa,
un qualsiasi graffio
mi strappa la pelle come cartaccia
e fa stillare sangue annacquato.

Ancora risaltano i punti
del desiderio sul mio corpo
ma il loro lume si sta spegnendo
e dove si originano
– testa gola e cuore –
si rifrange per un attimo un arcobaleno.

Se il sole è favorevole
il fagotto si sente intero.

MATRIOSKA

L'involucro più intimo
è la pelle,
mi affaccio ai suoi orifizi.

Poi i vestiti
che mi offuscano
o interpretano il mio lucore.

La casa è carapace
crivellato
dall'ansietà.

Città, paese, mondo
sono gabbie
condivise e cenciose.

Il clima è il gomitolo
più spazioso
che possa aderirmi,
luce e ombra i filamenti
del mio cielo.

La cipolla sente la spoliazione
dei suoi strati?
Grida il suo cuore?

Questa farfalla gialla
non si pela da nessun lato,
è puro essere.

ELEMENTO ACQUA

i
Il fiume nella sera tiepida
è il ritratto di una dimensione occulta
del mio corpo?
Nelle cascate il sangue scorre impetuoso
recuperando il ritmo di altri anni;
più giù scivola dividendosi
intorno a rocce e rami caduti
come vasi sanguigni del cervello
in cerca di illuminazioni;
nelle oasi dipinge il sogno.

ii
La corrente bianca fredda
attraversa i miei margini
penetra per i miei pori,
nell'impeto
nel calore del mio corpo
acqua e sangue diventano
una sola cosa
vena della terra.

iii
Dissanguatemi, vi prego,
tagliatemi il braccio destro
legandolo perché l'attività febbrile
cessi e la forza che aveva
scorra irrorando di rosso la terra
e mi lasci pallida e debole
senza più impegno con il desiderio.

IV

*A volte ci sembra che il misterioso in questo
mistero risieda in un malinteso, e che il malinteso
lo produca la nostra complicazione; senza sapere in che cosa consista,
presentiamo che dev'essere qualcosa di molto semplice, semplice come
le soluzioni della vita e dell'amore…*

VLADIMIR JANKÉLÉVITCH

ANCORA

i
La luce stagna nell'occhio,
i suoni si riducono a borborigmi,
lo scheletro fa circuiti
tra varie posture
in differenti punti
mentre il tempo trascorre incolore.

ii
Un ramo dalle foglie molto verdi
ha cancellato un velo,
all'improvviso il tempo è un altro,
la carne ha consistenza,
la luce è un istante rubato
al niente avvolgente
alla morte che attende.

ASTROLOGIA

Il calcolo delle influenze astrali
delle sue combinazioni e disgiunzioni
si dispiega all'infinito
quando il soggetto dell'oroscopo
non c'è più.

Il mare mosso degli appetiti
progetti sublimi o malvagi
illusioni in crescita
anche nella decrepitezza
trascina verso un futuro
che non esiste.

Il tempo incarnatosi negli organi
irregolare e spietato
rinchiuderebbe annunci della verità
ma è cieco e muto.

Ad ogni istante il mio essere
risuscita dall'abisso.

Fino a quando?

CREMATORIO

La pietra afferma il compimento
della mia anima minerale,
più dentro c'è solo il fuoco.

Non è inferno anche se lo abita
il buio cangiante
dell'occhio di Lucifero
e ruggisce come l'incendio
della città appestata;
aumenta e fa esplodere le febbri
e allora brilla come il forno per il pane
o il fresco sole del mattino.

Alla fine restano le braci
e la luce assoluta.

SENZA URNA

Soffiano venti spinosi
sulle torri del silenzio[3]
travolgono ceneri e capelli
sostengono le poderose ali
degli avvoltoi che si poseranno
per straziare il morto.

Braccia e gambe ardono
fieramente come la legna
quando la pira è alta
e sono abbondanti gli oli,
il fragore assorda:
olocausto di uno che culmina
nell'esplosione del cranio.

Avvolto in garze come una mummia
il corpo scivola dalla barella
e cade in mare.
L'acqua ammorbidisce il sudario,
il sale intenerisce la carne deserta,
resta il sacco d'ossa
sul fondo cieco.

La terra gettata cade
negli occhi spenti
invade la bocca socchiusa
schiaccia il petto
comprime i fianchi

---

[3]   Il riferimento è alle Towers of Silence, le strutture dove i parsi espongono in India i cadaveri per lasciarli alla cura finale degli avvoltoi. Tale pratica si chiama anche *sky burial*.

mentre la carne si illiquidisce
aiutata dai vermi
e si fa un'unica sostanza
con la terra.

Il quinto elemento
è lo spazio
tra le galassie
tra le particelle atomiche
di un fiore o di un cervello,
una simile quasi nullità
non ci avvicina all'aldilà?
Non sarà in questa fusione
la vita eterna?

L'universo non risponde.
Riempiamo lo spazio di angeli
e spiriti desideranti.

LA MORTE FUORILEGGE

La morte fuorilegge
giunge errabonda e ferita.

In una fenditura che si apre
tra il volto dell'oscurità
e l'ultimo battito
gemono voci intrappolate
si lamentano ridono amaramente
chiedono perdono o vendetta,
una registrazione animata nel vuoto.

Infelici le materie
che ricevono le lamentazioni,
si scuotono fino al midollo
e rischiano di cancellarsi.

I THANATOS

Signor Thanatos

Lei, signore, vive (o non vive)
in una frontiera fantasma
tra il nulla impensabile
e tutto il resto.

Forse che le dita dei suoi piedi
per una disattenzione non scompaiono
a volte dall'altra parte?
Come fa per ritirarle
– intere o decomposte –
su questa sponda dove lei non esiste
se non virtualmente?

Non nego il suo potere
nel coito nella preghiera nel pane
si installa la sua garitta
desiderandola o aborrendola
tutti andiamo lì.

Perfino la tigre.
Quando le si avvicina la meraviglia
di strisce incendiate e artigli fieri
lei non prova pena a spezzarla
contro quel muro ipotetico?

Il giorno che tocchi ai miei cani
(dis)conoscere l'ultimo cammino
li accolga per favore con affetto
li spinga dolcemente
verso quel silenzio.

LA CASA DI THANATOS

La casa di Thanatos si estende
su un piccolo promontorio
a pochi passi dal muro
di compatta oscurità.

Tesori e carabattole
ingombrano le stanze:
perle manoscritti scrigni
qualche scarpa graffiata
tonnellate di monete,
in una scuderia riposano animali domestici
e perfino neonati,
oggetti che gli agonizzanti
hanno voluto portarsi nell'oltretomba
e che si sono congelati qui
per la forza del desiderio.
Quelli che sono rimasti ai loro cari
non sono altro che delle copie.

Thanatos si gode i suoi mobili
affacciandosi alle finestre,
non ha tempo per entrare.
Non dorme mai.

LA SPOSA DI THANATOS

La sposa di Thanatos
dorme nella sua alcova,
il letto è morbido e fiorito,
il volto si affaccia da un nido
di seta e velluto,
lei respira gentilmente.

A volte la pelle liscia
e le palpebre dolci
sembrano quelle di una neonata;
poi le labbra arrossiscono,
i capelli vibrano sottilmente:
aspetta che la risvegli
la voce dell'amore?

Non si sa l'ora,
alla fine apre gli occhi
sul volto scuro e rugoso,
sorride con piena compassione
al passante stordito
come a dirgli il mio abbraccio
è la promessa che ti accompagna
fino al limite.

THANATOS, LA FAMIGLIA

Per quelli che trascina
una morte incontinente
senza decoro, senza tributi
Thanatos cambia la sua persona
moltiplica le sue apparizioni
figli improvvisi e provvisori.

Il *Thanatos nano* manda segnali
a paralitici e mutilati
a esseri che le guerre triturano
che vedono le loro stesse viscere:
in me confidate, grida,
io so che all'ultimo istante
di luce si restaureranno
le membra eroiche
la vista aperta.

Il *Thanatos terroso* si accoccola
offre la sua mano pelosa
a quelli che marciscono dentro
e non sanno che cosa gli succede
né conoscono dottori.
Benvenuti, cancri, dice,
benvenuti, funghi,
siamo tutti della stessa sostanza
che qui si illumina in pace.

Azzurro quasi trasparente
un *Thanatos piccolo*
germoglia nel mare
accanto al bebè che annega

giallo e curvo
per il bimbo che soccombe
attraversando il deserto.

Grigio piombo è il plotone
dei *Thanatos gnomi*
che assistono tra le rovine
di città bombardate.

Sfumano rapidi come si erano cagliati
rapidi come si estinguono
i brevi viaggi che scortano,
ciascuno il proprio senso.

V

SENZA...

Le ombre sono belle
nell'assedio del giorno
ubique compagne
che nulla esigono,
e che mi abbandoneranno.

La luce che risplende dentro un giglio
sulle vette all'imbrunire
tra i peli della gatta
i miei occhi la prendono in prestito
e non potrò mantenerla.

Il corpo si guasta,
il carro del destino cade a pezzi
mentre il cervello spegne sinapsi:
quando diventerà una massa grigia inerte
dove sarà la sua luce?

Senza ombre
senza fiore
senza cervello
un filo di luce

mi conoscerà?

MAREA TARDÍA

ROWENA HILL

LA LENTA DIGESTIÓN DE LAS PALABRAS

Nota sobre *Marea tardía* de Rowena Hill
Silvio Mignano

En un pasaje de *Il fu Mattia Pascal* (*El difunto Mattia Pascal*), novela de 1904 del escritor y dramaturgo italiano Luigi Pirandello, Premio Nobel de literatura en 1934; el protagonista, quien ya no se deja llamar Mattia Pascal sino Adriano Meis, atiende una puesta en escena de *Electra* de Sófocles interpretada por títeres automáticos. Mattia/Adriano se queda desconcertado por la novedad, que revela brutalmente el concepto de ficción en la tragedia clásica, e intenta imaginar lo que ocurriría si Orestes, en el momento en el cual está vengando la muerte del padre, se percatase de que el cielo es simplemente un telón de papel, y además desgarrado.

En *Salto*, el segundo poema de este nuevo libro de Rowena Hill, "al fondo del escenario de los días / detrás de un telón negro raído / gesticulan fracciones de figuras". Son sus antiguos maestros quienes le explican esas imágenes, o figuras, o fracciones de figuras, a la poeta, y agregan: "¿no sientes como jalamos tus cuerdas?". Justo, diríamos, como con un títere, con uno de los títeres que protagonizan la *Electra* a la cual asiste el difunto Mattia Pascal.

La ficción, en el sentido más borgiano, es el hilo común de *Marea tardía*. El mar no es el mar, es una construcción mental que se alcanza a través de una escotilla en un sótano: es un mar bajo el mar, agitado por corrientes y olas que mueven la memoria en el lector, obligándolo a pensar nuevamente en sus propias certezas existenciales, que ya no parecerán tan ciertas y firmes.

Asimismo, el ojo no es simple órgano de la vista en una perspectiva anatómica, si bien una ventana de la cual nos asomamos para ver à *rebours* nuestras vidas. Estas serán transformadas en piezas teatrales y sobre el escenario desfilarán zamuros, gatos, nubes, palomas y mariposas –títeres, una vez más, que no son los que aparecen sino otra cosa, personajes que encarnan sentimientos, memorias, fragmentos de la existencia.

Rowena Hill vive perteneciendo a dos idiomas, el inglés y el español, y en una pluralidad de culturas. En una realidad, la venezolana, que a su vez es un caldero de identidades y herencias humanas y culturales y a la vez eterna tierra de frontera entre mundos distintos. Escribe y traduce, Rowena, y entonces tiene una familiaridad única con la ambigüedad de la palabra, que es también su fuerza y riqueza. Una palabra no siempre tiene el primer significado que nos viene a la mente cuando la leemos y escuchamos, y nadie más que un traductor lo sabe.

Así, una bolsa de plástico azul que gira entre el polvo de una calle vacía no es necesariamente lo que creemos, puede anunciar una bandada de duendes demacrados que se apoderan de una ciudad hecha de escombro y desecho. Un sentimiento de profunda lástima recorre el libro, acompañado por el dolor que la memoria produce en lo íntimo de la poeta. Ella no tiene ningún pudor hipócrita en enseñarnos la añoranza por los instintos que aún viven en su cuerpo y que sin embargo ya no corresponden a lo que fueron: lo hace a través de versos que tienen una estructura simple, aparentemente banal, y que sin embargo son densos y a veces necesitan un tiempo largo para ser leídos de veras y sobre todo digeridos.

No es sin embargo una metamorfosis feliz, la que estos poemas filosóficos de Rowena Hill nos presentan: no hay solamente una reflexión catártica sobre la existencia y su transformación en el tiempo. La parte final del libro de hecho adquiere tonalidades desoladas: queda poco espacio para cualquier redención, en una realidad donde el crematorio es un horno de pan que brilla y la alternativa a la combustión es el deslizarse del cuerpo, sin urna, hacia la profundidad ciega del mar –una vez más, el mar metafórico que se abre en nuestras íntimas conciencias.

Es la expresión de un duelo ya no solo personal sino colectivo, donde las Torres del silencio de los Parsi en India se convierten en una titánica maquinaria fúnebre, una imposible camilla de cuya altura vertiginosa los cuerpos caen hacia el abismo. Entonces quizás no sea un titiritero quien maneje las cuerdas de los personajes en el escenario: puede que sean las Moiras y que su gesto sea más bien el de cortar los hilos.

Una síntesis poderosa entre las imágenes del titiritero y de las Moiras es Tánatos, que llega al final del libro como un verdugo y a la vez un libertador, sutilmente en equilibrio entre dulzura y violencia, tragedia y humor. La voz de Rowena Hill adquiere quizás en ese momento su nivel más alto: en el punto en el cual no hay fronteras entre los sentimientos humanos, donde el miedo y la esperanza se anulan y coinciden, dejando espacio a las más eternas preguntas existenciales, a la palabra y a su indefinible naturaleza proteiforme.

MAREA TARDÍA

I

MAR DE FONDO

La conversión

El arañar de ratas en el sótano
se vuelve percusión,
pulsos aleatorios en el fondo del mar
chocan y hacen temblar,
chispas dispersas se juntan
en un relámpago,
revelan la cara del dios
la mano con la daga.

Salto

Al fondo del escenario de los días,
detrás de un telón negro raído
gesticulan fracciones de figuras.
«Somos tus maestros», susurran,
«desde la infancia te enseñamos a escupir, a rezar,
¿no sientes como jalamos tus cuerdas?»

«No lo siento», respondo
y paso apartándolas
hacia una habitación vacía
donde el silencio es alarido
sin salida hasta que descubro
una escotilla en el piso.

Salto sin ver el suelo,
en la espesa oscuridad mis dedos tantean
semillas aladas de palabras.

Mar bajo el mar

En un sótano de la psiquis
un mar bajo el mar
iluminado por una luz mortecina,
de eclipse, en la playa
ningún ser vive.

Camino por el borde de las olas silenciosas
soñando el parto entre la espuma
de células y cantos.

De repente el agua se abre
y comienzan a salir arrojados
fragmentos de vidas y cuerpos
cables torcidos astillas de muebles
alas rotas peces ahogados
y piernas marchitas cráneos con hilachas
nudos de tripas y venas,
se retuercen y mueven sobre la arena.

Yo quiero, deseo
desde lo más profundo de mí
armar los escombros
recomponer los añicos
del mundo que me pertenece.
Pero soy inútil, muda
y en mi renuncia saboreo la paz
mientras la luz se disipa.

Yo me borro, pero ¿la luz?
No era amanecer, era crepúsculo,
se fue. Y ¿esos ojos
que irradian en el suelo?

Mar de leva

Agitación - dice el diccionario -
propagada desde el interior.
Llega a las playas en grandes olas
que amenazan los paseantes
y sacan a relucir
los fermentos del fondo.

LAS FLORES

He vivido las flores
perdiéndome en el corazón de sus trompas
traspasada por sus lanzas
brillando en sus soles.

Luego descendí por los tallos
y los troncos macizos,
nadaba en las mareas de la savia.

Y ahora con las raíces
me hundo en el barro de la fuente
el oscuro humus que germina
y descompone.

HACIA LAS ENTRAÑAS

Quiero volver al sótano
que me pertenece.
La gata se acuesta a mi lado,
la pulcritud del pelo anaranjado y blanco
me atrapa, bosteza
y la porcelana puntiaguda
de los dientes marca el canal
hacia la garganta oscura.

Acudo al diccionario de sánscrito,
una palabra -*vyoman* - me pasea
por objetos y dimensiones
- cielo y agua, vaca y joya,
lo absurdo de una flor que crece en el aire -
de una vida intensa remota,
las letras y su resonancia
me hunden en la tierra negra
donde germina el lenguaje.

PENSANDO EN SÁNSCRITO

Las hojas de la palabra hoja
son un segundo nacimiento,
detrás están los trapos verdes venados
mudando con los sesgos de la luz.

****

Lidiando con la sintaxis
aturdido por las conjugaciones
el ojo de repente percibe
cómo una ballena enorme
surge del mar de los sonidos
que buscan enunciar,
constelándolos.

****

Cualquier letra de un alfabeto
separada mascullada con asombro
conduce a la piel del mismo cuerpo
infinitamente denso preñado
tóxico del lenguaje.

****

Las hojas que caen sin nombre
las nubes que desfilan vaporosas
por el ojo demente o extasiado
llevan al mar abierto
pura liquidez sin orden
sin tiempo, terror
o gozo animal.

LOS POLACOS

para Igor Barreto

Disponerse a ascender
el K2 en invierno,
desear una temporada de dolor
 tan puro e intenso
como las estepas de nieve
blanca hasta la médula de los huesos
hasta las paredes internas del cráneo
más allá de toda certeza
o esperanza:

¿equivale a la valentía
del poeta que abre el cuerpo
a todas las desgracias humanas
y de su época aciaga
articulándolas como rocas en el entorno
 de la cima escondida
el bien incólume?

II

EL NUDO

La primera sustancia
el parto espontáneo
sin causa o relación
de la nada madre
es la luz.

Hasta generaciones sin número
incuba en las células
de todas las criaturas,
conversa con la luz del cielo.

Los ojos son su puerta.

En el momento de la muerte
cuando se zafa el nudo del pecho
y las estructuras se desarman
¿lo que quedará será de nuevo la luz libre?
¿a eso nos reducimos:
luz esencial y sin fronteras?
o ¿desandamos el último pasaje?
¿se anula con uno el principio
en la nada?

TESTIMONIOS DEL OJO

La ventana

Yo soy el ojo
soy lo único que no veo
en un día sin nubes rastreo el horizonte
miro trepar los zarcillos de una vid
o madurar las espinillas bajo una barba.

Al revés veo subir la bilis
en el cuerpo que me sostiene
y la arquitectura proliferante de los sueños.

Soy bisagra
soy membrana
soy cámara
a veces me canso demasiado
puedo volverme opaco en los dos sentidos
algún día voy a girar y cesar.

TRÍPTICOS

Las tres partes del mismo instante ovoide
dividido en nombre del intelecto
en fuera dentro y pantalla
deben ser devueltas a su cáscara
amalgamadas sin costuras
para que la luz allí abunde
y la memoria enraíce.

El ojo encuentra el mundo,
formas y texturas
profundidades y movimientos
imprimen su constelación única
en la retina blanda,
perfectamente recibida
la llama de esa coyuntura
es libre del tiempo.

Los nombres se adhieren
puede ser un nanosegundo más tarde,
luego manos pecho cabello
y poderosos pies,
dioses y diosas
convierten los elementos en historias
someten amor y miedo.

El ojo tiembla en la corriente
que sopla desde corazón y nervios
 percibe el flujo de jugos
sus oscilaciones
y los colores que emanan de las vísceras.

olas agolpadas
azul se quiebra blanco
el viento azota

Su reposo se interrumpe
se agita molesta
escupe reproches
en la garganta
del perturbador.

Una marea íntima
crece y bulle
con vetas carrasposas.

zamuro parado en la cumbrera
cabeza pelada rotando
alas tendidas al sol

Ángel negro
el zamuro descansa
de su oficio de carroñero
 su hambre que purga.

La repulsión por su calvicie
 arrugada y gris
se disuelve en simpatía
por sus gestos de persona.

crepúsculo en el borde del jardín
margaritas amarillas retienen
la claridad del día

Las flores brillan como faroles
para insectos rezagados
tienen todavía a raya
las tinieblas.

Asombro hondo
aplauso del corazón
por la luz que florece
contra la noche.

el viento mece la selva
hojas sueltas revolotean
hacia el piso moteado

Un aliento antiguo
domina los árboles
cambiando estaciones
como claves en la música.

Los gestos de una danza
punzan y suben por las extremidades
sacuden con el asalto del otoño.

el gato mira
sus ojos son círculos
brillantes y quietos

Un pequeño dios
fija el objeto
el pelo puede temblar
las uñas contraerse
la mirada es inmóvil
piedra vidente.

La mano que busca la suavidad
por el irrespeto puede ser arañada,
los músculos tensan y se aflojan.

moto destrozada
tirada bajo el camión
mancha que se expande sobre el asfalto

¿Desde dónde en el pasado
halaba el Destino los hilos
de esta colisión?
¿Vio el conductor
caer la espada?

La carne se encoge y trema
frágil y blanda
presiente el impacto
de metal arrojado.

las nubes trazan
estrías en el cielo
de margen a margen

Una mano de artista
ha cubierto la bóveda
de plumas blancas.

La vista se alza,
corazón y aliento
se arrojan tras ella
al espacio espumoso.

apiñados en filas
hombres y mujeres esperan
en la calle inmunda

Un diosito falso
gordo y fofo
los ha condenado a anaqueles vacíos
y la dieta de mentiras.

La lástima encoge
el corazón,
la vergüenza se mezcla con rabia
por la impotencia.

secuencia de figuras exactas
se posa una paloma
en una cornisa

Las formas que usó dios
para articular la creación
triángulo círculo cuadro
alternan de muro en muro,
el vuelo de una paloma
perturba esta simetría.

Envidien la tersura del ave
la libertad para aletear
sin saber que habita
el esplendor.

una cucaracha moribunda
cáscara brillante marrón
agita patas débiles

La especie diseñada para durar
un millón de años
descarta sus miembros
crujientes bajo los pies
y se multiplica
y se multiplica.

Pica el asco
en nariz y labios,
se dan escalofríos en vientre y muslos,
la compasión se desprende,
el pie se prepara para pisar.

una bolsa de plástico azul
gira entre el polvo
de la calle vacía

Los dioses desertaron,
la ciudad pertenece ahora
a los duendes demacrados
de los escombros y desechos.

Un hueco en el vientre
abre y traga
la fe en el futuro
la alegría diaria.

un escarabajo iridiscente diminuto
se aferra a una rosa amarilla
devorándola

La vida se alimenta de vida,
así lo estableció
un creador ambivalente
su noción de equilibrio.

El corazón se rebela pero sabe
que esa fiereza íntima
es una especie de amor.

III

DUELO

Mi casa ya no es
mi casa, refugio, roca
habitación en torno a una fuente;
sus guardianes mudos huyeron
al caer el último árbol del lindero
abatido por los invasores;
la esfera transparente reventó,
flotan los añicos de su silencio
sobre el jardín árido,
caen de noche en el techo,
pasos de un animal herido.

El órgano elástico
que era yo se ha rasgado,
se acartonan los gestos
de una danza dispersa.

El sueño de redondez que traje
se fragmenta, deja el hueco,
a veces se reconoce en una astilla.

BOLSA DE HUESOS

Acuesto la cabeza,
no siento la suavidad
de mi carne acolchada
que se funde con el cojín
sino un contenedor duro
que no encuentra reposo.

Salto y los resortes
de mis piernas no amortiguan
el traqueteo de la bolsa de huesos,
cualquier arañazo
rasga el papelacho de mi piel
y mana una sangre acuosa.

Se marcan aún los sitios
del deseo en mi cuerpo
pero su lumbre se está apagando
y en los puntos de generación
- coronilla garganta corazón -
se refracta por momentos un arco iris.

Si el sol favorece
el bulto se siente entero.

MATRIOSKA

La envoltura más íntima
es la piel,
me asomo en sus orificios.

Luego los vestidos
que me ofuscan
o interpretan mi brillo.

La casa es caparazón
acribillada
por ansiedades.

Ciudad, país, mundo,
son jaulas
compartidas y harapientas.

El clima es el ovillo
más espacioso
que se me adhiere,
luz y sombra las hebras
de mi cielo.

¿La cebolla siente el despojo
de sus capas?
¿Chilla su corazón?

Esta mariposa amarilla
por ningún lado se pela,
es puro ser.

ELEMENTO AGUA

i
El río en la tarde tibia
¿es retrato de una dimensión
oculta de mi cuerpo?
En las cascadas la sangre fluye rauda
recobrando el ritmo de otros años;
más abajo se desliza partiéndose
en torno a rocas y ramas caídas
como los vasos del cerebro
que busca iluminaciones;
en los remansos pinta el sueño.

ii

La corriente blanca fría
 atraviesa mis linderos
 penetra por mis poros,
 en el ímpetu
en el calor de mi cuerpo
agua y sangre se vuelven
una sola cosa
vena de la tierra.

iii
Sángrenme les ruego,
corten mi brazo derecho
atándolo para que la actividad febril
cese y la fuerza que llevaba
mane rociando de rojo la tierra
y me deje pálida y floja
sin compromiso con el deseo.

IV

*Algunas veces nos parece que lo misterioso
de este misterio reside en un malentendido,
y que el malentendido lo produce nuestra complicación;
sin saber en qué consiste, presentimos que debe ser algo muy simple,
simple como las soluciones de la vida y del amor...*

VLADIMIR JANKÉLÉVITCH

TODAVÍA

i
La luz se ha estancado en el ojo,
los sonidos se reducen a borborigmos,
el esqueleto hace circuitos
entre varias posturas en diferentes puntos
mientras el tiempo transcurre incoloro.

ii
Una rama de hojas muy verdes
borró un velo,
de repente el tiempo es otro,
la carne tiene consistencia,
la luz es un instante robado
a la nada envolvente
a la muerte que espera.

ASTROLOGÍA

El cálculo de las influencias astrales
sus combinaciones y disyunciones
se despliega hasta el infinito
mientras el sujeto del horóscopo
ya no está.

El mar de fondo de las apetencias
proyectos sublimes o malvados
ilusiones en crecimiento
aún en la decrepitud
arrastra hacia un futuro
que no existe.

El tiempo encarnado en los órganos
irregular y despiadado
encerraría avisos de la verdad
pero es ciego y mudo.

A cada instante mi ser
resucita del abismo.

¿Hasta cuándo?

CREMATORIO

La piedra afirma el cumplimiento
de mi alma mineral,
más adentro sólo está el fuego.

No es infierno aunque lo habita
lo oscuro tornasolado
del ojo de Lucifer
y ruge como el incendio
de la ciudad apestada;
crece y revienta las fiebres,
entonces brilla como el horno del pan
o el fresco sol de la mañana.

Al final quedan las brasas
y la luz absoluta.

SIN URNA

Soplan vientos espinosos
sobre las torres del silencio
arrasan células y pelos
sostienen las poderosas alas
de los buitres que se posarán
para desgarrar el muerto.

Brazos y piernas arden
tan fieramente como la leña
cuando la pira es alta
y son abundantes los óleos,
el fragor ensordece:
holocausto de uno que culmina
en la explosión del cráneo.

Envuelto en lona como una momia
el cuerpo se desliza de la camilla
y cae al mar.
El agua ablanda la mortaja,
la sal enternece la carne desierta,
queda el bulto de los huesos
sobre el fondo ciego.

La tierra arrojada cae
en los ojos apagados
invade la boca entreabierta
aplasta el pecho
comprime los flancos
mientras la carne se licúa
asistida por los gusanos
y se vuelve una sola sustancia
con la tierra.

El quinto elemento
es el espacio
entre las galaxias
entre las partículas de los átomos
de una flor o un cerebro,
tan casi nada
¿no nos acerca al más allá?
en esa fusión
¿no estaría la vida eterna?

El universo no contesta.
Llenamos el espacio de ángeles
y espíritus deseosos.

LA MUERTE MALANDRA

La muerte malandra
llega desamparada y herida.

En una franja que se abre
entre la cara de la oscuridad
y el último latido
gimen voces atrapadas
se quejan ríen amargamente
piden perdón o venganza,
una grabación animada en el vacío.

Infelices las materias
que reciben las lamentaciones,
se sacuden hasta los tuétanos
y arriesgan borrarse.

LOS TÁNATOS

Señor Tánatos

Usted, señor, vive (o no vive)
en una frontera fantasma
entre la nada impensable
y todo el resto.

A veces los dedos de sus pies
en un descuido ¿no desaparecen
en el otro lado?
¿Cómo hace para retirarlos
- enteros o descompuestos -
a esta orilla donde no existe
sino virtualmente?

No le niego su poder,
en el coito en el rezo en el pan
 se instala su garita,
deseando o aborreciéndolo
hacia allá vamos todos.

Hasta el tigre.
Cuando se le acerca la maravilla
de rayas encendidas y garras fieras
¿usted no siente pena en quebrarla
contra ese muro hipotético?

El día en que les toque a mis perros
(des)conocer el último trayecto
acójalos por favor con cariño
empújelos suavemente
hacia ese silencio.

LA CASA DE TÁNATOS

La casa de Tánatos se extiende
sobre un pequeño promontorio
a escasos pasos del muro
de oscuridad compacta.

Tesoros y cachivaches
abarrotan las habitaciones:
perlas manuscritos cofres
algún zapato rayado
toneladas de monedas,
en un establo descansan mascotas
y hasta bebés,
objetos que los agonizantes
quisieron llevarse a la ultratumba
y aquí se congelaron
por la fuerza del deseo.
Los que quedaron a los deudos
no son sino réplicas.

Tánatos disfruta sus muebles
asomándose a las ventanas,
no tiene tiempo para entrar.
No duerme jamás.

LA ESPOSA DE TÁNATOS

La esposa de Tánatos
duerme en su alcoba,
la cama es suave y floreada,
el rostro asoma en un nido
de seda y terciopelo,
respira bajito.

A veces la piel lisa
y los párpados tiernos
son de recién nacida;
luego los labios enrojecen,
el pelo vibra sutilmente:
¿espera que la despierte
la voz del amor?

No se sabe la hora,
al fin abre los ojos
en la cara morena arrugada,
sonríe con compasión entera
al transeúnte aturdido
como diciendo mi abrazo
es la promesa que te acompaña
hasta el límite.

TÁNATOS, LA FAMILIA

Para los que arrastra
una muerte incontinente
sin decoro sin tributos
Tánatos cambia su persona
multiplica sus apariciones
hijos súbitos y provisorios.

Tánatos enano hace señas
a lisiados y mutilados
a seres que las guerras trituran
que ven sus propias tripas:
en mí confíen, grita,
yo sé que en el último instante
de luz se les restauran
los miembros heroicos
la vista abierta.

Tánatos terruño se agacha
ofrece su mano peluda
a los que se pudren dentro
y no saben qué les pasa
ni conocen doctores.
Bienvenidos cánceres, dice,
bienvenidos hongos,
somos todos de la misma sustancia
que aquí se alumbra en paz.

Azul casi transparente
un *Tánatos chico*
brota en el mar
al lado del bebé que se ahoga

amarillo y jorobado
para el niño que sucumbe
en la travesía del desierto.

Gris plomo es el pelotón
de los *Tanatoses gnomos*
que asisten entre escombros
de ciudades bombardeadas.

Se esfuman tan rápido como cuajaron
tan rápido como se extinguen
los breves viajes que escoltan,
cada uno su propio sentido.

V

SIN...

Las sombras son hermosas
en el cerco del día
ubicuas compañeras
que nada exigen,
y me abandonarán.

La luz que resplandece dentro de un lirio
sobre los picos al atardecer
entre los pelos de la gata,
mis ojos se la prestan
y no podré sostenerla.

El cuerpo se estropea,
el carro del destino se desmorona
mientras el cerebro apaga sinapsis:
cuando se vuelva una masa gris inerte
¿dónde estará su luz?

Sin sombras
sin flor
sin cerebro
¿una hebra de la luz
me conocerá?

CONTENTS

LATE TIDE | ROWENA HILL

Made in Miami Beach ~ Printing as needed

◊◊◊

2021

www.ingramcontent.com/pod-product-compliance
Lightning Source LLC
Chambersburg PA
CBHW020156090426
42734CB00008B/844